TABLE OF CONTENT

- Note Sheets at the beginning of each Lesson

- Lessons Worksheets

- Answer Sheets

LESSON 1
ARE YOU READY?

HAVE FUN LEARNING AND GROWING !!!

Listen, Learn and take Notes

Listen, Learn and take Notes

Listen, Learn and take Notes

Are you Ready?

DEFINE THESE WORDS
WEAPONS * KINGDOM OF GOD * WARFARE

you will need chapter one from Teach us to War book

....

....

....

....

....

....

....

....

....

Answer these Questions

1. WHY DO GOD GIVE US WEAPONS OF WARFARE?

you will need chapter one from teach us to war book to answer these questions

....

....

....

....

....

....

....

....

....

2. NAME A WAY YOUR EFFECTIVE IN SPIRITUAL WARFARE?

use chapter one from teach us to pray to answer questions

....

....

....

....

....

....

....

....

....

WHAT BIBLE VERSE GIVES MANKIND GOD'S ORIGINAL MANDATE?

use chapter one from teach us to pray to answer questions

....

....

....

....

....

....

....

....

....

4. WHAT BIBLE VERSE STOOD OUT TO YOU AND WHAT DID YOU GET FROM IT?

....

....

....

....

....

....

....

....

....

You got it!

Job well done!

....

....

....

....

....

....

....

....

....

....

....

LESSON 2

Holiness: offense and defense

HAVE FUN LEARNING AND GROW!!

Listen, Learn and take Notes

Listen, Learn and take Notes

Listen, Learn and take Notes

Holiness: offense & defense

DEFINE THESE WORDS
OFFENSE * DEFENSE * HOLINESS

You will need chapter two from Teach us to War book

....

....

....

....

....

....

....

....

....

Keep going!

....

....

....

....

....

....

....

....

....

....

....

FILL IN THE BLANK

You will need chapter two from Teach us to War book

It's ok to _____ _____

_____

Holiness gives us the _____ to

_____ the _____ and make him

_____

Holiness allow us to do what effectively? (according to chapter 2)

_____ and _____

WHAT BIBLE VERSE IN TEACH US TO WAR CHAPTER 2 STOOD OUT TO YOU AND WHAT DID YOU GET FROM IT?

....

....

....

....

....

....

....

....

....

Great Job!

Your doing it!

LESSON 3

Build and War

HAVE FUN LEARNING AND GROWING!!

Listen, Learn and take Notes

Listen, Learn and take Notes

Listen, Learn and take Notes

ANSWER THE QUESTIONS

You will need chapter three from <u>Teach us to War book</u>

1. What are the 2 main ways satan tries to stop us?

----

2. In 2Timothy 1:7 what God has not given us and what did he give us?

----

3. WHAT DID YOU LEARN OR WHAT STOOD OUT TO YOU IN NEHEMIAH 6:1-23?

....

....

....

....

....

....

....

....

....

Your doing well!

Awesome Job!

LESSON 4 PART 1:

What's Your Weapon of Choice?

HAVE FUN LEARNING AND GROWING!!

Listen, Learn and take Notes

Listen, Learn and take Notes

Listen, Learn and take Notes

Part 1: What's your Weapon of choice?

DEFINE THESE WORDS
ARSENAL ✱ GRACE ✱

you will need chapter 4 part 1 from Teach us to War book

....

....

....

....

....

....

....

....

....

ANSWER THESE QUESTIONS

you will need chapter 4 part 1 from Teach us to War boo[k]

1. WHAT ARE YOUR SPIRITUAL WEAPONS OF CHOICE?

----

2. WHAT WEAPONS YOU BELIEVE GOD ASSIGNED YOU? (IT'S OKAY IF YOU DON'T KNOW, YOU WILL COME TO KNO[W]

----

3. HOW DO WE GET PUBLIC VICTORY?

---

4. WHAT DID YOU LEARN FROM 1SAMUEL 17: 26-51, AND WHAT DO YOU BELIEVE GOD IS SAYING TO YOU THRU THESE VERESE ?

Your doing Good!

....

....

....

....

....

....

....

....

....

....

....

....

Job well done

....

....

....

....

....

....

....

....

....

....

....

....

LESSON 4 PART 2:

Using your Weapons, the Right way

HAVE FUN LEARNING AND GROWING!!

Listen, Learn and take Notes

....

....

....

....

....

....

....

....

....

....

....

....

Listen, Learn and take Notes

Listen, Learn and take Notes

PART 2: USING YOUR WEAPONS, THE RIGHT WAY

Answer these questions
you will need chapter 4 part 2 from *Teach us to War* bo[ok]

1. WHAT HELPS YOU WITH CHOOSING YOUR WEAPON OF WA[R]

----

2. IF YOU DON'T KNOW YOUR WEAPON HOW DO YOU FIND OU[T]

----

3. NAME THREE SPIRITUAL WEAPONS?

WHAT WEAPON WHEN USED THE RIGHT WAY WILL CAUSE GOD TO COME TO YOU?

WHAT WEAPON GOD USE TO HELP US, AND WHAT IS HE SENDING WHEN HE USES THIS WEAPON?

LESSON 5

Let's War: its war time

HAVE FUN LEARNING AND GROWING!!

Listen, Learn and take Notes

Listen, Learn and take Notes

....

....

....

....

....

....

....

....

....

....

....

Listen, Learn and take Notes

LET'S WAR: IT'S WAR TIME

Answer these questions
you will need chapter 4 part 2 from Teach us to War bo

1. WHY ARE BATTLES BEING LOST?

----

2. HOW DO WE WIN?

----

3. HOW DO SATAN WIN?

WHAT 3 THINGS WE DO TO START BECOMING A WARRIOR?

5A. BEING IN THE SPIRIT OF GOD EQUAL WHAT?

5B. BEING IN THE FLESH EQUALS WHAT?

CONGRADULATIONS YOU FINISHED

ANWERS SHEETS

nly to be looked at to check answers after completing each lesson

TO DEFINE ALL WORD CORRECTLY ALL DEFINITIONS SHOULD BE TAKEN FROM TEACH US TO WAR BOOK

nswers will vary but what's underlined should be mentioned and in same contexts

....

LESSON 1 ANWERS

All answer can be found in Teach us to War book, expect the questions asking you what your learned

....

1. to <u>win</u> the battle <u>against the kingdom of darkness</u> and for the <u>expanding</u> of <u>the Kingdom of God</u>

....

2. <u>Following God's Rule</u>

....

3. <u>Genesis 1: 26-27</u>

....

4. pick a scripture from chapter 1 and wrote what you learned and what stood out to you.

....

ANWERS SHEETS

only to be looked at to check answers after completing each lesso[n]

TO DEFINE ALL WORD CORRECTLY ALL DEFINITIONS SHOULD BE TAKEN FROM TEACH US TO WAR BOOK

answers will vary but what's underlined should be mentioned and in sa[me] contexts

....

LESSON 2 ANWERS

All answer can be found in Teach us to War book, expect the questions asking you what your learned

....

1. <u>need God help</u>

....

2. <u>power, resist, devil, flee</u>

....

3. <u>war and damage against the kingdom of darkness</u>

....

4. pick a scripture from chapter 2 and wrote what you learned and what stood out to you.

....

ANWERS SHEETS

Only to be looked at to check answers after completing each lesson

TO DEFINE ALL WORD CORRECTLY ALL DEFINITIONS SHOULD BE TAKEN FROM TEACH US TO WAR BOOK

Answers will vary but what's underlined should be mentioned and in same contexts

···

LESSON 3 ANSWERS

All answer can be found in Teach us to War book, expect the questions asking you what your learned

···

1. <u>personal attacks</u> and <u>purpose assign attacks</u>

···

2. God <u>has not given</u> us a <u>spirit of fear</u> but of <u>love</u> <u>power</u> and <u>sound mind</u>

···

3. wrote what stood out and what you learned from Nehemiah 6: 1-23

ANWERS SHEETS

only to be looked at to check answers after completing each lesson

TO DEFINE ALL WORD CORRECTLY ALL DEFINITIONS SHOULD BE TAKEN FROM TEACH US TO WAR BOOK

answers will vary but what's underlined should be mentioned and in same contexts

···

LESSON 4 PART 1 ANSWERS

All answer can be found in Teach us to War book, expect the questions asking you what your learned

···

1. <u>picked your three Spiritual weapons of choice</u>

···

2. wrote the Spiritual weapons you believe God has assigned/given to you

···

3. <u>listen,</u> and <u>following God's instruction in private</u>

···

4. wrote what you learned from 1Samuel 17: 26-51 and what you believe God is saying to you thru them verses.

···

ANWERS SHEETS

Only to be looked at to check answers after completing each lesson

TO DEFINE ALL WORD CORRECTLY ALL DEFINITIONS SHOULD BE TAKEN FROM TEACH US TO WAR BOOK

Answers will vary but what's underlined should be mentioned and in same contexts

....

LESSON 4 PART 2 ANSWERS

All answer can be found in Teach us to War book, expect the questions asking you what your learned

....

1. <u>Knowing what way God graced you</u>

....

2. <u>ask God to reveal them</u>

....

3. <u>named three Spiritual weapons</u>

....

4. <u>Praise</u>

....

5. <u>Angels</u> and <u>Supernatural Aid or Assistance</u>

ANWERS SHEETS

only to be looked at to check answers after completing each lesson

TO DEFINE ALL WORD CORRECTLY ALL DEFINITIONS SHOULD BE TAKEN FROM TEACH US TO WAR BOOK

answers will vary but what's underlined should be mentioned and in sar contexts

....

LESSON 5 ANSWERS

All answer can be found in Teach us to War book, expect the questions asking you what your learned

....

1. <u>fighting spiritual warfare in the natural/flesh</u>

....

2. <u>Surrending our will to God and submitting to God's will</u>

....

3. <u>keeping us in the flesh</u>

....

4. <u>1 come into the righteousness of God thru Jesus Christ</u>
<u>2 learn to war God's way</u>
<u>3 following God's rules</u>

....

5a <u>countless Victories</u>
5b <u>countless defeats/loses and death</u>

CPSIA information can be obtained
at www.ICGtesting.com
Printed in the USA
LVHW071927200422
716761LV00002B/8